MW01534459

Otherworldly
Tales
I've Been Told

by

Ed Kelemen

Copyright 2016 by Ed Kelemen

ISBN:1534667733
ISBN-13:9781534667730

All rights reserved.

No part of this book may be reproduced, stored in a retrieval system, or transmitted in any form, by any means electronic, mechanical, photocopyhing, recording, or otherwise without the express written consent of the author.

Published in The United States of America by
Nemeleke Publishing
New Florence, PA
2016

Dedication

This book is dedicated to all those who have had experiences outside the realm of normality and have been brave enough to share them with me. Thank you.

Acknowledgments

A book is never the accomplishment of a single individual and this one is no different. Without people like C. William Davis III, "Mr. Ed" Gotwalt, Warren A. and Bethannie M. Mack, Joanne McGough sharing their experiences, as well as those who wished to remain anonymous, these stories would never have been told.

My undying gratitude goes out to the members of the Greensburg Writers Group, a little gathering of clinically insane people who have had the patience over the past decade to gently critique my meager attempts at scribbling.

And the cover art. What can I say about it. It is yet one more example of the great artistry of Linda Ciletti who has the uncanny ability to catch the essence of a book with her great designs.

Foreword

I have written many articles and stories about the paranormal and the supernatural. In my books *Pennsylvania's Haunted Route 30, Pennsylvania's Haunted Route 22, Weird West Overton,* and *Haunted Foothills,* I have been able to verify each and every incident.

However, when I am at various events speaking and/or doing book signings, I encounter many people from all walks of life. Frequently these people share their own personal paranormal experiences with me. For various reasons, lack of time chief among them, I am unable to personally verify the stories. But the people relating their experiences are just everyday persons like you and I. They have no ulterior motive in sharing their stories and even, for the most part, wish to remain anonymous to avoid unpleasant interactions with non-believers. But, since I have personally witnessed their sincerity and have no reason to doubt their veracity, I feel compelled to share these stories with you.

Table of Contents

Otherworldly Tales I've Been Told

Premonition, Prediction, or Clairvoyance?

One afternoon at a book signing, I was approached by an elderly gentleman who introduced himself as Max and said that he thought he might have, "ESPs." Since I know at least one certifiable genius who can't pronounce the word "serif" properly, I found no humor in his misuse of the word.

With a little prodding, he told me what had happened to him and his family one day a few years back.

Max had a beautiful daughter by the name of Marcelline who was blessed with someting sorely lacking in today's youth – a work ethic. Instead of spending her free time chained to a game console, an MP3 player, or sending endless texts on an iPhone, she went out and got a job.

Since she was a high schooler, it was a minimum-wage job at a local fast food restaurant where she spent a lot of time flipping burgers and making fries.

"Marci would always tell me that maybe it only paid minimum wage, but it was a lot more than she would get for sitting on the couch watching TV," Max said.

Nevertheless, every night when she came home from her shift, she would spend a long time in the shower getting the smell and feel of grease from her hair and off her body.

I could see Max's pride in his daughter when he told me that, from time-to-time, he would chide her for using too much water or shampoo. It was a private joke between the two of them.

One evening Max fell asleep watching TV. He usually didn't do this, but he had had a tiring day at the loading docks. So, after dinner he plunked himself in his recliner and had a beer while scanning the day's headlines in the paper. Even though it was a morning paper, Max preferred to read it at night.

Well, by and by, Max nodded off and the paper fell to his lap.

Max didn't remember falling asleep or dreaming anything for a while. Then he had a nightmare. He heard his Marci screaming over a vat of hot grease that had splashed her face when she put a batch of fries into it. The nightmare faded and didn't awaken him.

He was awakened by the sound of the telephone on the stand next to his recliner. And he knew who it was before he even answered it.

"Hello."

"Mr. --------, do you have a daughter named Marcelline?"

"She's been burned hasn't she? What hospital is this? I'm on my way."

As things worked out, Marci wasn't burned badly, just a few spots on the side of her face and her left ear. And they healed nicely without even leaving a scar.

The only question that Max had was to ask me, "If I had wakened earlier, could I have saved my little girl the pain she went through?"

I confessed that I didn't know, but probably not. I told him that he was probably witnessing it as it happened and he couldn't have done anything about it.

I don't know if that was the right answer, but it made both of us feel a little better, and isn't that what it's all about?

Mr. Ed's Ghost

Mr. Ed's Elephant Museum and Candy Emporium appears as an explosion of color along the Lincoln Highway when approaching Gettysburg from the west. Travelers from the west cannot count it as a trip to Gettysburg unless they stop in and say hi to Elly the Elephant and enjoy the indoor and outdoor display of over 12,000 pachyderm figures of all sizes and shapes. Did I mention the candy? Candy, candy, candy of every kind – I once even saw beer-flavored jelly beans. Home-made fudge to die for that'll satisfy even the most discerning palate is made right there by Cheryl, Mr. Ed's Chief Fudge Maker.

Is there actually a Mr. Ed? There sure is! Ed Gotwalt is the founder and patriarch of the business and has become a beloved Gettysburg celebrity. He is rightfully famous for his philanthropy, always giving back to the community. Mr. Ed sponsors free concerts and activities on-site weekly during the summer. His free 5,000-egg Easter egg hunt vies with his free visit with Santa where each kid receives a free gift from the jolly old elf in popularity with area kids.

What's all this got to do with ghosts? Not much, unless you want to count the one that shares Mr. Ed's home with him.

For some reason or another, Mr. Ed and other members of his close-knit family smell the unmistakeable aroma of Cherry pipe tobacco being smoked in his smoke-free home. Neither he nor any of his family members can recall anyone that actually smoked a pipe in the house.

Of course Gettysburg is known as one of the most haunted towns in all of the country. So, perhaps it is the spectre of a long departed Civil War soldier who had a particular penchant for cherry-flavored pipe tobacco. However, I don't know when cherry pipe tobacco was even developed, so it could just as easily be a farmer or townsman who passed on at some post-war year.

Who it might be is a matter of speculation

and, until he makes an appearance, we can only guess from the not-unpleasant aroma of that sweet smelling pipe smoke.

Transformation of a Non-Believer

I was exchanging pleasantries with a young lady who had spent at least as many decades on this planet as I when we switched the topic from the intricacies of flax scutching to health care. It seems as though people of our age are fascinated with anything that has to do with extending our lives.

All this talk of mortality naturally led to interacting with people who had come to the end of their lives. Some people call them ghosts; others call them spirits. Whatever they are called, a lot of people refuse to acknowledge their existence. We've all heard variations of their denial time-after-time, usually stated thus: "There ain't no such things as ghosts!"

She introduced me to her husband of many years who confessed to being one of the nay-sayers when it came to ghosts. He said he was vociferous in his denial of the existence of an afterlife on this plane of existence. He had never seen a ghost, so they must not exist, right?

I had no desire to enter into a no-win conversation, so I just nodded my head. I wasn't agreeing with him, I was just acknowledging that I had heard him.

Then he said, "until" and I started paying attention again.

And here's the story of his conversion in his own words, starting with that attention grabbing word:

Until the wife and I stayed at a place near Lancaster, PA called the Smokehouse Inn, room number seven, to be exact.

When we checked in, the desk clerk apologized, explaining that the only room left was number seven

I asked what was wrong with room number seven and was told nothing really, just that some people who stay there complain.

"About what?" I asked

"The ghosts," he replied.

"Yeah right," I told the clerk, "Just get us checked in. I'm sleepy."

Later that night, after the wife and I settled in, she poked me in the arm.

"Do you smell that? She asked.

"Smell what?"

"Horses," she replied.

Smell them I did. It wasn't overpowering. It was faint, as though a horse had been in the room some time ago and left a lingering odor. It wasn't even unpleasant to someone like me who grew upon a farm.

"I'll complain to the desk in the morning," I told her.   And promptly forgot about it.

Later on she poked me again.

"Do you smell that?" she asked.

"Smell what."

"Horses."

"No," I told her.

"See?" She asked and rolled over and went to sleep.

The next day, Saturday, we made the obligatory tour of the Lancaster area Pennsylvania Dutch attractions. Ate at a humongous buffet, bought things that we would never have a use for, went for a hay ride, and "oohed and awed," at all the hex signs on the barns.

When we finally got back to the Smoke House Inn after dark, we were ready for a hot shower and a night in the comfy bed. We were flat out exhausted and didn't even want a late night cocktail. So, we went to bed.

But not to sleep.

Someone was right outside the door to tour room talking. Not loud enough to understand the words, but loud enough to interrupt our sleep. How rude! After a while, I got out of bed and went to the door. The talking went on and I yanked the door open to remonstrate them about their lack of courtesy. There was nobody there.

After looking up and down the hallway to be sure it was empty, I closed the door. The talking resumed and I yanked the door open again with the same results. On about the third, or maybe fourth time, the talking didn't stop. It went on in the hall outside the door with me standing there. But, just like the other times, I was the only one in the hall. I don't need to tell you, I was just a bit spooked.

I went back inside that room number seven and slammed the door hard enough to wake my wife, even though I didn't eally mean to. She asked me what was going on.

After I told her, she said, "See?" then rolled over and went back to sleep.

But I didn't. Fully awake, I just lay there, staring at the dark ceiling and trying to make out the words in the spectral conversation just outside the door of our room.

Next thing was heavy footsteps clomping along the hallway. They always ended just outside the door to the room. Until the time they didn't.

I wasn't scared, just a bit annoyed with the prank being played on me.

Then the footsteps approached my door again. Only this time whoever it was walked right through the door and tromped into the room, ending right at the foot of our bed.

I saw the semi-solid apparition of a man dressed in the uniform of a Civil War soldier, but I couldn't tell whether it was a Confederate or Union uniform. The large, dirt covered man with the tangled beard pinned me in place with an evil stare that made me thnink he wanted *me* out of *his* room. And the definite aroma of a horse came right along with him. I remembered thinking that he should have at least had the common decency to scrape his boots before entering the room. That thought didn't last long. I was overcome with fear. reached over and poked my wife until she awoke.

"Whaa...?" She mumbled, clearing the sleep from her eyes.

Then she saw the ghost at the foot of the bed. She sat up in the bed and we watched him as he faded away into nothingness.

I told his wife everything that happened leading up to the apparition walking through the door, arriving at the foot of the bed, then standing there in an accusatory manner.

She said, "And?"

I told her, "Honey, I've been wrong all these years! I'm sorry. I promise I'll never doubt you again."

She asked me, "Even the snow globe story?"

I replied, "Even the snow globe story."

Well, this got my attention again, so I asked, "what is the snow globe story?"

...And this brings us to our next tale of the supernatural...

The Snow Globe of Death

Now that her husband had admitted not only the possibility of, but the actual existence of an afterlife and other things beyond his immediate knowledge and without the presence of empirical proof, she told me the story of the snow globe.

In her own words -

When I was a young girl, I lived in the country. We had a small, bare existence farm. We were what you might call poor, but we didn't know it. Daddy worked at the mine when work was available and Mom made all our clothes. Granny did most of the cooking. The ground wasn't good enough for us to grow much more than just enough of a crop for ourselves, our chickens, and one nearly dry old cow.

The older folk along with my two sisters and I were all crammed into the old frame 2-story farm house on a few acres of hardscrabble land.

Granny sometimes got some money from folks for her curing and skrying. She had "the gift." People would come from all around the valley for Granny's help.

I guess that some people nowadays might call her a witch, but she wasn't. She just wanted to help people however she could. You see, she knew all about herbs and stuff like that.

When someone was having problems with their pregnancy, Granny was there to help with one of her potions. When that pregnancy came to term, she was always people's first choice as a midwife. She helped bring dozens of children into the world.

Nagging coughs, fever, stomach problems, headaches, woman's problems, sprains, strains, and what-have-you, Granny fixed 'em all. She could sew wounds and splint broken bones. That wasn't all, either.

Granny could "fix" other things as well.

Young girls came to her for help in attracting true love and men came to her for help with nagging wives. Farmers asked her help with the weather, and couples asked for help with fertility.

Once in a while someone would ask for help with a particularly pesky problem. Like the farmer that complained that his neighbor was stealing some of his pigs and chickens. Mr. Hendersen wanted the thief cursed, but Granny wouldn't do that. She never wanted to hurt anybody.

So she wrapped herself in a shawl, took a little bag of ingredients for her potions and went to the suspected thief's farm and had a visit.

While there, she mentioned that some pigs and chickens had recently turned up missing in the area and wanted to warn him and others about those animals in case they should wander onto their farms. Now, I don't know what, exactly, Granny told him about the animals. All I know is that about a week later Mr. Hendersen stopped by with a fat piglet that he gave to Granny with his thanks for her help.

Now, all of Granny's efforts didn't have happy endings. Having the "gift" she could sometimes see things that she rather wished she didn't. For instance, there was the young girl who found herself in the, "family way." Not only was she husband-less, she didn't even know who the father might be, although she had narrowed it down to two young fellows. She wanted Granny to name the father so that he could do the "right thing" by her.

Granny got out her skrying bowl, put some liquid in it along with a secret potion of hers. After lighting a candle, she then covered her head, the bowl, and the candle together under her shawl. She mumbled something in a sing-song voice while under there for what seemed an extraordinarily long time. Eventually, she uncovered herself, the bowl, and the candle announcing, "There's nothing I can do for you sweetie. You lied to me."

Later that night I overheard my Mom and Granny talking. Mom said, "You know who the father is, don't you?"

Granny replied, "I do."

"Why then didn't you tell that poor girl?"

Granny said, "Oh that girl knows who it is. She lied when she swore that she had only been with two men who could have gotten her in that way."

Granny continued, "All I can say is that her baby is going to bear a mighty resemblance to her brother."

"I see," Mom said. It was never mentioned again.

`Another time a couple brought a baby boy to Granny. It was a sickly little thing, definitely off its feed, coughing and feverish. They asked for Granny's help.

Granny wrapped the baby in her shawl and put it in the middle of Mom and Dad's bed. She sprinkled a little powder over it and said some prayers. Then, she asked to be alone with the baby for a while and we all left the room.

Ten or so minutes later and she came out of he bedroom, tears streaking her face.

"There's nothing I can do," she told the distraught parents. "It's beyond my abilities to help. Nature will run its course."

Then, we all said a prayer for the little one that its short time on this earth be without any more pain. But of course, it was. I think the prayer was more to make the little boy's parents feel better that it was for him.

One question they had for Granny was, "How long does our son have?"

"You have a snow globe on your mantle, don't you?" she asked.

"Why yes, but how did you know that?" the mother replied.

"It makes no difference how I know. Just know that that snow globe has a small leak in it. When all the water in it runs out, you son will no longer be with you."

And Granny would say no more.

A few months later, I found out that their baby had perished in early spring, just as the world was being reborn from its temporary winter death.

When the young couple returned to their home, the husband inspected the snow globe and found the teeny-tiny leak at the bottom. He figured that he could cheat Fate by sealing the leak, which he did with some pine rosin. And, it sat in its place of honor on the mantle leak free.

But, even though he was hanging on, their son deteriorated all through the winter. He was a pitiful little soul, in pain and crying a lot. When the weather started to change, he perked up a bit and they thought he was going to be fine. The little homestead was brightening after the long winter, just was nature itself was doing.

Then, one day in mid April, the wife heard the family dog going berserk out on the front porch. Running to see what was the matter, she opened the door and saw that the dog had cornered a squirrel where the porch roof meets the house.

"Stop it now, dog," she commanded. "He just a small fellow and not even worth shooting. Let him grow up and we'll eat him later."

With that, she shooed the dog away with her broom.

Just then, the squirrel clambered down the porch post and headed for his tree, but the dog saw him and lunged in his direction barking.

The squirrel darted through the opened door, the dog inches from its bushy tail, barking like there was no tomorrow.

She chased both of them trying to corral the animals and get them out of the house, but they ran all over the first floor. The squirrel was adeptly running over, under, and around things without running into anything. The dog was another story. He ran into chairs, knocked stuff off the table, and caused chaos everywhere he went.

Finally, the squirrel lighted on the mantle and the young mother edged toward it, hoping to shoo it off and out the door. Just then the dog leaped for the squirrel, clearing off the mantle in the process.

The snow globe hit the floor, burst open and all its contents leaked out.

That night, the little baby boy who had been baptized Lazarus passed away.

You can't cheat Fate.

Years went by and Granny passed on.

More years went by and Mom also passed on. They tried to teach me their ways, but either I was a lousy student or I just didn't have "the gift." But I do have some abilities to commune with spirits of folk who have left us for another realm of existence. Especially when I wear Granny's shawl.

Domestic Relations Don't Ensure Domestic Tranquility

If you take a ride along Manor Drive in Ebensburg, PA you will be rewarded with some of Pennsylvania's most beautiful scenery along the winding road through the rolling countryside. As you travel along, watch the right side of the road. At 499 Manor Drive you will see a complex of buildings on that side. The rectangular three story red brick building is the home of Cambria County's DRC, or Day Reporting Center.

The Day Reporting Center program is one that is designed to help alleviate recidivism within the county's criminal justice system and to more smoothly reintegrate convicted offenders back into society. Persons allowed into the DRC program are required to report every day, in person, to complete a three-level treatment program that is specifically designed for each client. Not only does the program give the clients life skills and understanding that allows them to become productive members of society, it also costs quite a bit less per client to the taxpayer than incarceration.

The DRC program was started in May, 2013 and shows great results in rehabilitation. After a bit of shuffling here and there, it settled in the ground floor of that old red brick building which is also the home of the Cambria County Domestic Relations Office.

The Domestic Relations Office is responsible for, "all matters establishing the paternity for children born outside of marriage and in establishing and enforcing financial and medical support for minor children and, if appropriate, dependent spouses." Their words, not mine.

OK, what does all this have to do with anything?

Well, a friend of mine got caught up in the slow moving, grinding wheels of justice a while ago. After serving 90 days in the county lockup, he was admitted into the DRC program which meant that he had to report and take classes six days a week as he moved up through the three levels of treatment.

He usually had a bit of time on his hands while waiting for the public bus service to make its stop at the DRC for the hour-long trip back to Johnstown some 25 or so miles away. During this time, he made the acquaintance of a number of the maintenance workers at the facility. After a while, when he had gained their confidence, they began to tell him stories about that old red brick building.

The evening cleaning crew has had some experiences in there that don't quite fall under everyday happenings.

One day, the conversation turned to these occurrences. It went like this:

"Did you know that this building is haunted?" One of the workers asked him.

"No way!" he replied.

"Yes way. I've heard things myself," the worker came back with. "Things like heavy footsteps clomping along the hallway upstairs where the Domestic Relations Offices are."

"Yeah," another of the maintenance staff

chimed in, " And what about those arguments and fights that take place up there all the time at night when there is supposed to be nobody there?"

"We are supposed to be the only ones in the building after hours," the first worker said. And he went on, "But sometimes it sounds like there are a whole bunch a people running around and arguing and fighting up there."

"And when we first heard it, we used to run up there to see what was going on. And there would be nobody there."

The second guy added, " What about all the times we go up there and someone, or something turns off the lights?"

"Right you are," the first worker came back. "And how many times have we heard the radio playing up there only to have it turn itself off when we enter the hallway?"

The two workers then snubbed out their cigarettes, patted my friend on the back and took his leave, telling him that they'd see him again the next day.

Is the building haunted? Maybe, but not by

spirits. If it's haunted by anything, it's by the raw and intense emotions that are played out at Domestic Relations on a daily basis. Emotions that are so bitter, vehement, and harsh that they get imprinted into the very building itself, only to be played back when calmness and quietude settles in the velvety darkness of the night. Velvety darkness that insures that anybody who encounters them will be spooked.

Babies Crying From the Beyond

Over the years I have refrained from including the old Monsour Hospital in my writings as a haunted location, even though it has been well-known locally as a site of paranormal activity. "Why so?" you might ask.

Simple, because publicly-accessible places that are known to be hotbeds of paranormal activity draw the attention of those who are less than scientific in their approach to "ghost hunting." Usually young people with noting to do on an evening who treat it as a lark and leave vandalism, destruction, and beer cans in their wake. You need go no farther than to witness the vandalism of graves at Livermore Cemetery by those too unintelligent to realize that it was actually never in the movie, *Night of the Living Dead.* That and the complete destruction of the Amity Hall Hotel in central Pennsylvania by a trio of arsonists trying to smoke out the haunts during a bit of drunken revelry. Then, there is the possibility of youngsters being severely injured in unstable structures. Regardless of how you or I feel about this kind of activity, permanent paralysis or death is not the proper punishment for a bit of youthful indiscretion. After all, we have all been guilty of things that aren't ranked high on our lists of prideful accomplishments.

The Monsour Hospital was never provided with a guard and was only protected by an easily defeated chain link fence. That it was a dangerously unstable structure is demonstrated by the fact that, during demolition of the hospital in February, 2016, an entire section collapsed upon itself and onto the adjacent busy US Route 30 next to it. This east-west arterial highway was completely blocked for hours on multiple days while the debris was cleared.

Now that it is gone, I can offer you the following account of activity there by retired nurse and author of the *Tommy Two Shoes* series, as well as a large number of other stories, Tom Beck, who says the following:

"I worked at Monsour for a year before changing hospitals. In the old hospital their surgical intensive care unit was directly above the morgue. I was told that during the night shift, nurses in the unit would often hear babies crying. These nurses were very credible witnesses and I had no reason to doubt what they were saying. I didn't work the night shift often and only rarely worked in the surgical intensive care unit, so I can't confirm what they had heard.

"This hospital was located along a busy four lane highway. The road ran right past the front door of the emergency department. Accident victims were often brought into the emergency room for treatment, no matter how severe the injury.

"It was highly likely that babies and children, as well as adults had died in those accidents and were placed in the morgue until the coroner would release them. At that time there were no air rescue helicopters to fly survivors and some victims would die because the advanced care of larger hospitals wasn't readily available.

"The deceased were brought to the hospital as well. The coroners requested that the dead be taken to a hospital to be pronounced by a physician. Most hospitals have stories of ghosts, spirits and of unexplained sightings or sounds."

Further future investigations will need to be done to determine if the spirits have gone the way of the hospital or if they are bound to the grounds of the former healing facility.

A Hungry Ghost?

This tale goes back generations and was told to me by an octogenarian who said that her mother told her the story. Furthermore, it was at a meeting of church ladies, so I just *know* that it must be true. Here's what she had to say -

"Back in my childhood days, we children liked to roam all over the hills and valleys around our little rural town. It was back in the day when we had a hotel and train station right in town next to the feed mill. The bridge across the Conemaugh was about a quarter mile downstream from where the new bridge is now. The old bridge got washed away in the big flood.

"Anyhow, there's this big old hill that overlooks the valley a little ways south of town. It's called Squirrel Hill. I don't know why, I never saw any squirrels up there, just lots of rabbits. Now, somewhere's or another up there, an Indian chief is rumored to have died. How he died isn't really known, but most people said that he starved to death during a nasty winter.

"Like I said, as children we liked to roam all over that place. It was a good berry-picking place and we liked to go up there, have a little campfire, and spend the night from time-to-time.

"Well, it never happend to me, but my mother says it happened to her brother a long time ago. You see, if you sleep on that hill all night and get up in the morning and start to cook over the campfire, you will hear the old Indian chief moaning like he was in pain or something.

You won't see anything, but you can hear him clear as a bell. After a while, if you ask him what he wants, he will say, "Breakfast." And if you throw a bit of what you are cooking into the underbrush, he will stop moaning and leave you alone."

I assured her that I would never venture up on Squirrel Hill without an extra Egg Muffin for the hungry Indian chief.

Granny in her Rocker

An older fellow related this one to me:

"I'm from Butler County here in PA and have been for all my life. Same with my wife. Let me tell you something that happened a few years ago.

"It was in the late 1990s or thereabout and my wife's momma had taken ill, so we went over to her house a lot to care for her. One particular day I had worked all day cutting firewood and was just about completely out of energy.

"Well, you see, her mom lived in the old family home on the family farm that had been in the family for generations. It went back to before the Civil War. It was a big ole two story frame thing with add-ons and covered porches and all.

"That particular day when I was dog tired, we went over to help out as best we could and make her mom comfortable and bring her some food. If I remember right, she had a touch of some kind of flu or something. Anyhow, while the missus was upstairs tending to her mom, I decided to relax on the couch downstairs. I think I had the TV on, but I don't remember that for sure.

"I must've drifted off to sleep, cause the next thing I knew, I was woke up by the sound of the old rocking chair creaking back and forth on the wood floor over by the front window.

"I rubbed my eyes and looked over there and saw a really old lady just rockin' back and forth, back and forth, smiling and looking out the window. She was wearing a dress with a apron and a little cloth covering her hair.

"I called over to her to see if I could help her or something and, right before my eyes, she disappeared, just like that! She looked at me, smiled and faded away.

"I ran upstairs to my wife and mother-in-law and told them all about it.

"They told me not to worry about it, it was my wife's grandmother's favorite chair and she still likes to rock away in it from time-to-time.

Rosie and Mac

Rosie waited for Mac to come home. It was late, she had already put the two little ones to bed. It wasn't like him to be late. Mac always tried to schedule his week so that he left the big rig at the depot early enough to be home for supper come Friday night. There was never a lot of money, but she always tried to have something special for his Friday night dinner, the first home cooking he would get since Sunday afternoon.

She didn't realize how much she missed him until it got close to the time for him to be home. She absolutely loved it when he burst through the kitchen door, swept her off her feet and smothered her with kisses as he spun her around. Then he spoiled the girls with whatever gifts he was able to pick up on his weekly five night over-the-road journey. It was never anything big, just something so that they knew he thought about them while he was away. They adored their daddy.

Likewise, she adored her husband, companion, lover, protector, confidant, and anchor.

After the girls settled down and went to sleep, she cleared the table, wrapped the food, and put it away so it wouldn't get stale. Someting must have happened, but it would turn out alright. It always did. There was the time that he got stuck in a snow storm in Montana for four days. She remembered once that he got diverted back to Texas and missed an entire weekend at home. Then there was when the truck broke down in Vermont and he had to wait for repairs to be done. He'd call whenever he got to a phone.

She sat alone at the kitchen table chain-smoking and drinking tea. Life wasn't easy in the Allegheny Mountains for a twenty-three year old mother of two married to an over-the-road truck jockey. They were just starting out in life in a six room fixer-upper on 10 acres. Much better than the cramped 3 rooms they had in town before he got on with the trucking company.

She thought of their song, the one Patsy Cline sang on the radio,

"Oh, we ain't got a barrel of money,

Maybe we're ragged and funny.

But we'll travel along

Singin' a song

Side by side."

She drifted off to sleep right at the table with her head cradled in her forearms, the song still echoing in her mind,

"I don't know what's a'comin' tomorrow

Maybe it 's trouble and sorrow

But we'll travel the road

Sharing the load

Side by side."

As she slept, she entered dreamland and her husband came to her in that state, standing right at her side next to the kitchen table.

"Baby." That was his favorite nickname for

her. He always said that if Lauren Bacall could be Bogie's baby, she could be his.

"Baby – wake up. I need to tell you some things."

She rubbed the sleep from her eyes and looked up at him. He wasn't wearing his regular big smile. He looked downright serious.

"Wha- what's the matter hon?" She asked.

"Nothing Baby. I just want you to know that you're going to be alright."

"I know that, silly. I have you to take care of me."

He shook his head from side to side. "No Baby, this is serious. I want to tell you some things."

She nodded and he went on. "My life insurance policy from the trucking company is in the bureau drawer with all my important papers. And the military life insurance that I took out when I got discharged is with it. Between the two of them there is over $40,000. Plus, I took out loan insurance on our mortgage, so the house and property will be paid off. Got it?"

She nodded again and said, "Honey, what's wrong. You're scaring me."

He shushed her and said, "I don't have a lot of time to finish this, so I need you to listen. If you're careful with it, the money from the insurance should last you and the girls until you get the farm up and running. And I don't want you to spend a lot of money on the funeral..."

She interrupted, "What funeral?"

"Baby, please just shut up and listen. I don't want buried in no fancy duds, just some clean blue jeans and my favorite green flannel shirt. I never wore a suit and tie in my life and I sure don't want to wear 'em for eternity."

She was speechless as the import of his conversation dawned on her. He went on, going so far as to tell her exactly what casket he preferred (the cheapest one). "... and don't let no mealy-mouthed undertaker switch you into something more expensive. It don't matter if I'm buried in a casket made of wood or in one of gold, it's all the same to me." He told her who he wanted for pall bearers and who he thought would give the most honest eulogy, "the Lord knows I weren't no saint, so don't make me out to be none."

Wide eyed with just the hint of tears starting to form, she nodded again.

Like I said, Baby, you're going to be alright." And with a kiss on the tip of her nose, he faded from sight.

"Through all kinds of weather

what if the sky should fall?

As long as we're together

It doesn't matter at all."

*

The raucous ringing of the phone intruded on her dream.

She snatched it from its cradle and answered it saying, "Honey, I just had the strangest dream about you. Wait'll I tell you about it."

But it wasn't him. It was her mother-in-law.

"Rosie, your phone's been out of order or something. People've been trying to get you for over an hour. Get up and get dressed. Mac's been in an accident. The hospital called and said we have to get there as soon as we can. I'll pick you up in 20 minutes."

"Did ... did ... did they say if it was serious?" she stuttered.

"Yes, they said it is serious."

*

People commented on how composed she was making arrangements and tending to all the details of the funeral. If she wept at all, it was in private.

When both the undertaker and her in-laws balked at burying Mac in jeans and a flannel shirt, she stood her ground, saying, "It's what Mac told me he wanted."

Same thing when some of the relatives felt they would be more appropriate pall bearers than the ones chosen.

"Take it up with Mac," she said.

Ed Kelemen

Ghost at Sam's Club?

I was spending a pleasant early spring afternoon with a group of fellow writers when Corey D. mentioned the following experience that he and his late father had:

"My Dad and I were shopping at a Sam's Club Warehouse in a suburb of Milwaukee, Wisconsin. As usual, we walked up and down the aisles loading our cart with far too much of things that we really didn't need. It just seemed a shame to pass-up a deal on things. So again, as usual, we had survival quantities of paper towels, hot sausage, potatoes, tomato sauce, aluminum foil, and so on in that cart. We were ready for the Apocalypse.

"Eventually we found our way to the household cleaner aisle and were standing sideways in the aisle talking about whether we really needed a giant box of steel wool pads.

"A slight movement about ten feet away caught our attention and I turned to my right while my dad, facing me turned to his left. What we saw was a super-sized bottle of Lysol move directly from its shelf about 4 feet over the cement floor and parallel to the floor until it was approximately in the middle of the aisle. Then it dropped directly to the floor with enough force to burst open and the contents spread out evenly in a perfect circle on the uneven concrete floor.

"What do you think?"

I confessed that I actually had no opinion on the incident. But maybe, just maybe, an otherworldly denizen was unsatisfied with the cleanliness of the floor in that particular location and decided to take action to rectify the situation.

Strange things happen.

Spirits Attached to Antiques

It was a hot summer day that 4th of July weekend at Twin Lakes Park. I was set up in a quiet wooded lane along with a number of other authors. The afternoon sun had dwindled the crowd, sun dappled the ground under the shade trees, and I was absorbed in watching the dust motes dance in the rays of that sun. All that, combined with a fresh mug of Arnold Palmer-style iced tea meant that I wasn't paying much attention to my surroundings. Another ten seconds and I would have been dozing.

My somnolence was interrupted by a slight cough and I returned to reality with a start. A nice family stood at my table and introduced themselves. They were an elderly couple and a middle-aged son. We talked about this and that for a bit and then the lady asked if I would be interesting in hearing the family's experience with spirits.

Of course you know I said "yes" and this is what she related to me.

" When I was first married to my husband, we bought an old house and moved into it as newlyweds. It was one of the first houses ever built in Fort Allen. It was definitely a fixer-upper, but we saw it, not as it was, but as it could be. Besides, we just knew that it would be an ideal location for all the antiques we intended to buy as furnishings and decorations.

"Things progressed nicely and we had great fun restoring the old dowager to her original beauty. After many, many months of scraping, sanding, painting, scrubbing, wiping, digging, and planting, we were finally satisfied with our labor of love. Of course, that didn't mean our work was done. There is always something to do in a building that old.

"Over the years we acquired a plethora of what we like to call "seasoned furnishings." Some people called them antiques and a lot of people called them junk. Our weekend adventures usually involved digging through stuff at yard sales, garage sales, flea markets, and roadside antique stores.

"The first years of our marriage also blessed us with a son.(Here she introduced him to me).

"But as time went on, we started noticing some strange occurrences in our gem of a home. It started off innocently enough, just the random knock-knock, groan, and creak. We just figured it was the sounds an old house makes, you know just like an old man with arthritis.

"I became concerned when my young son started asking me about the lady in the green dress. At first I blamed it on a youngster's imagination, you know – like having imaginary friends. But he insisted that she was real and she definitely wasn't a playmate. He said that she came and went at odd times, never on any kind of schedule. He saw her in the upstairs hallway and sometimes coming and going from one of the rooms up there.

"A few months later, my husband confessed that he also saw a lady walking around the house and property. His description however, was better. He described her as a young woman of about 30 or so years old, small built, and about five feet tall. She was wearing a white dress with a thingy on her head that he described as a doily. I think he meant that she was wearing a dust cap. He got the impression that she was wearing lace-up boots and she had curly brown hair in the style of a young Shirley Temple.

"He said that he usually saw her in the back park of the first floor where the big kitchen was located and sometimes walking around out back in the garden.

"So far, I hadn't seen anything like the men of the family had seen. Plus, the spirits or whatever they might have been didn't seem dangerous or anything. They just seemed gentle spirits wandering around. I actually thought it was kind of cool to have ghosts in my house. It gave me something to brag about to my less fortunate friends. If only I had known...

"Then it was my turn. One morning I went into the downstairs bathroom. I noticed someting splattered on the wall over the tub. It was brown and looked like it had run a bit. Mumbling something about messy guy, I got some Pine Sol and cleaned it up.

"I mentioned it that evening at dinner. Both my husband and son denied having anything to do with it. Curious.

"The very next day, that splatter was on the wall again. This time, I looked more closely at it and determined that it looked like nothing so much as blood. So I scrubbed it off again and that night chided the men for a not very nice practical joke. Again I was met with denials.

"Well! You can be sure that I checked that bathroom wall first thing the next morning. And – nothing. Then day after- again nothing. And every day I checked there was nothing there. I figured that the practical joke had worn thin and they stopped doing it.

"Then one morning two weeks later it was back! I saw the blood-splatter all over the wall just as it had been before. This time, there was going to be no denial. I left it there!

"When my husband and son arrived home for dinner, I escorted them into the downstairs bathroom and said, "Now, just which one of you is responsible for this?"

"They asked in unison, "Responsible for what?"

And the blood spattered wall was perfectly clean. As though it had never been stained. I was baffled."

She went on to explain that she contacted a psychic who did an investigation at her home. The psychic said that she helped the spirits of the two women cross over and that they wouldn't be back. As far as the blood splatter on the wall, she had no idea where it had come from, but suspected that it may be connected to one or another of the spirit ladies. When she asked, the psychic told her that the spirits of the ladies weren't connected with the house, but probably had been attached to one of the antiques she had brought into the house.

And, ever since, there has been no paranormal activity in the house.

She then purchased one of my books for a little girl she knew named Heather. I autographed the book with a short message to

Heather, gave it to her, and looked down to make change for the purchase. When I looked up they were gone. Now I had a clear view of at least 100 feet in both directions and could see them neither to the right nor to the left.

Curious.

The Haunted Television Set

It is fairly unusual although not unheard of, for a relatively new building to be haunted. Such is the Wyngate by Wyndam located on Route 30 across from the Arnold Palmer Airport in Latrobe, PA. After all, it was only opened for business at the turn of the century in 2000 to take advantage of the rapidly expanding airport.

A former maintenance and cleaning employee told me about a haunted room at the hotel. Actually, it was a haunted television set, one of the new flat screen ones. You see, it had a disconcerting habit of turning itself on and off at random times. Sometimes the guests would be awakened by the roaring volume of the TV which had somehow tuned itself to an action movie. Other times, just at the most important turning point of a movie, sporting event, or show, it would shut off, preventing the guests from knowing how it turned out.

The television set was removed and sent to a repair shop that could find nothing wrong with it. It was replaced in the room and resumed its antics. Only when the TV was removed from the room and replaced with another did the aberrant behavior stop.

When asked, the former employee told me he had no idea what happened to the television set. However, knowing what I do about how hotels dispose of unwanted items, there is someone somewhere in the area who has acquired a "bargain" TV that has a mind of its own. Perhaps an insomniac who doesn't mind loud TV shows in the wee hours.

Maybe it only gets "Chiller" channel.

The Energy Vampire

During one Halloween Season I happened to give a talk at a library not too far from my home. As usual, my topic was hauntings and folklore of Pennsylvania. In the audience was a young lady whose pretty and pert appearance caught my eye. And the way she was paying attention to my utterances was quite flattering to this particular septuagenarian.

After the talk I sat at a table autographing books for those who wished to purchase them.

When the meager crowd petered out, she approached me and asked, "Do you believe in vampires?"

"You mean the kind of vampires popularized by Abraham Stoker in the 19th century? If so, the answer is no. Dracula was a pure invention of his imagination, even though he was based on a real person. Vlad Tempe, also called Vlad the Impaler, Vlad Dracul, and Dracula, was a minor warlord who became famous for his penchant of impaling those he considered criminals along the road leading to his stronghold."

I was demonstrating my knowledge of the basis for the fictitious vampire. After all, it isn't often that I get to do so.

She indicated that the blood sucking, sun sensitive ghoul wasn't what she had in mind.

So, not wanting to give up the limelight, I continued, "Then do you mean the life-sucking, emotional and spiritual draining kind of vampire? Of course I believe in that type of undead beast. Anyone who has dealt with an ex-spouse's divorce attorney is familiar with that kind of vampire."

No, that wasn't what she meant, although I was getting close.

"I mean the energy vampire," she stated.

I ran down the various energy vampires that I was familiar with. This included all those electronic devices around the average home that are always in what is called "stand-by mode."

Some of these, particularly the box that controls home cable or satellite access, can use as much electricity as a refrigerator. I also mentioned desktop computers, printers, and so on.

"No, none of those." And she continued, "I am an energy vampire."

She went on to explain that she was born without the internal cellular structure that allows humans to convert food sources into life-sustaining energy. I'm not sure, but I think she mentioned either a gene or a chromosome that was lacking in her DNA.

She also mentioned that she hasn't a heartbeat and can win bets in a bar by challenging others to find one on her.

Even as an infant she learned how to glean energy from her surroundings. She would drain energy from batteries, electrical devices, and other living beings. For that reason, she was unable to have pets. While merely sitting and petting a kitten or a small dog, she would drain so much energy that the poor animal would expire.

With other humans, her very touch would

drain enough of their life force that they would need to sleep immediately to recoup what she had absorbed.

She had tried to have a normal life, fell in love, and was married. But after a relatively short time, her husband divorced her, even though the two were in love. You see, every time she touched him, he would become extremely exhausted and need to sleep. As time went on, her touch caused him to pass out on the spot as his life force was not being replenished enough between encounters. Fearing for his very life, he divorced her.

She now lives alone with her malady, gaining life force when she brushes against others or "accidentally" bumps into them at places like the mall. That way, she feels that she won't repeatedly drain any one individual. She couldn't live with the guilt that would bring.

With that she announced her intention to leave, saying, "I am sure you understand why I won't shake your hand."

She was right.

Sometimes a Bargain Isn't

A fellow at a rural location related the following to me:

"I was building an addition to our house and needed some building materials. Not too far from me was a business that had been demolished after a nasty fire. The demolition contractor was selling various items that he had salvaged from the building. Things like doors, some windows, light fixtures, roof trusses and concrete blocks.

"It was the concrete blocks I needed and the price was right, about a fourth of what I'd pay for new blocks.

"When I brought the load home, a friend of mine cautioned me about them. The original building burned down because it was cursed for being built over an Indian burial ground. And that the blocks may bring the curse with them.

"I just pooh-poohed that idea and went ahead with my addition, using the concrete blocks to make up the first story walls.

'Ever since I finished the project, it seems that a spirit has taken possession of the lower level of the addition and does anything he or she can do to irritate me, stuff like opening the basement door when nobody's home, stealing paper towels and scattering them on the floor, spilling small cans of paint – things like that."

He then asked me what he should do. I told him to get in touch with a Native American shaman, explain his situation, and ask him if he could and would perform a purification rite to appease the spirits of the ancestors.

Hairy Chests and Missing Money

After years of hospice nursing, author Joanne McGough retired from the hectic city life in and around Pittsburgh. She now resides in beautiful Laughlintown, Pa at the foot of Laurel Mountain with her collies, Tanya and Rocky and the feline boss of the house, Daisy. When not composing cozy page-turners like *A Bed and Breakfast Affair*, she spends time doting over her children and grandchildren, as well as tending her flowers and catching up on her traveling and cooking.

As a young wife and mother, Joanne lived in a stately, 100-plus year-old Gothic style frame house in the Pittsburgh suburb of Swissvale. Her family grew and the house was filled with the joyful sound of young girls playing, running up and down the stairs, and just generally getting into those things that youngsters are apt to.

That's about the time she noticed that things had a way of disappearing in the house. Nothing important, mind you, but it was a minor irritation. Things like keys, bobbins and needles, grocery lists, and so forth. And these things never stayed missing for an extended period of time. They always showed up in a while, but usually someplace other than where they had last been seen. Joanne always attributed these happenstances to a faulty memory or to someone else in the home moving them and then forgetting about it. No big thing, but mildly aggravating just the same. In addition to things being moved about, Joanne also had an uneasy feeling that she was being constantly watched in her own home, even when she was supposedly the only one there.

Brendan was the family's big ole friendly Irish Setter who had been named after Brendan Behan, the famous Irish Republican author. Now he had taken to raising his hackles and growling at a particular corner in the living room when nobody was in that corner.

One day, Joanne placed fifty dollars in the form of two twenties and a ten in a drawer. It was to buy groceries. Fifty dollars back in those days wasn't exactly considered chump change.

Imagine her consternation when she returned to retrieve that money and it was gone. This time it was no memory slip or inadvertent misplacement. It was theft, pure and simple. She questioned her husband thinking he might have needed it for car repairs or some such. Nope, he had nothing to do with the missing money. Likewise, the girls all expressed denial and no knowledge of the money's whereabouts.

The missing money was a blow, but life went on and she put it out of her mind, only remembering it occasionally.

The following summer she decided that the house was in need of a complete cleaning, top to bottom. Part of that included removal of the carpets to send them out for cleaning. When the carpet was rolled up in the room where the money had gone missing, fifty dollars consisting of two crisp twenty dollar bills and one ten dollar bill were lying smack dab in the middle of the floor that the carpet had covered. Numerous pieces of furniture had had to be removed to roll up that carpet and it wasn't within the ability of any one single person to do it.

It was the missing fifty dollars, no doubt about it. That's when Joanne realized that someone or something other than living human beings was sharing the house with her family. And she was going to do something about it. She called in a reader.

When Joanne mentioned the petty and sometimes not so petty thievery that had been going on for the past year or two, the first thing the reader asked was, "Are there any young girls in the home?"

When Joanne told her about her young daughters, the reader told her not to worry. Oftentimes, when girls are maturing into young women, they attract the attention of just such an imp as has been making his presence known by moving things about. It isn't really anything evil, it just wants attention. It'll go away as the girls grow a bit older.

Then she went on, "What about the big man with the hairy chest?"

"Big man with a hairy chest? Don't know what you're talking about," Joanne replied, but then rememberd that uneasy feeling of being watched.

"Oh yes, there is the spirit of a large man with a hairy chest in this house. I get the impression that he is either the previous owner or the builder of this house. He isn't malevolent, he just wants to make sure that his house is being taken care of properly."

When Joanne later mentioned this to her husband, Ed, he said, "Oh yes, I've seen him a couple of times in the upstairs hallway. And one time he was standing alongside the bed just looking at me."

Joanne wanted to know, "Why didn't you tell me?"

Ed told her, "I didn't want to scare you."

Back to earlier that day when the reader continued, "But I wouldn't worry about anything here anyway. You're not going to be living here that long."

"Huh?" was all that Joanne could muster as way of reply.

"I get the feeling that you or your husband

is going to inherit a new home. I see red brick and particularly, a pink kitchen."

Sure enough a scant year later, a relative of her husband passed away leaving them a brick duplex. And when Joanne entered what was to be their new home for the first time, she was struck by the clean and tidy *pink* kitchen.

The Gibson Girl Comes Home

C. William Davis III, Bill to his friends, is an author and speaker of some renown. His mystery series featuring Clive Aliston, a no-nonsense sheriff who solves unsolvable crimes in and around the gritty manufacturing center of the Steel City, Pittsburgh, has received both critical acclaim and popular success.

In 1974 Bill moved his family into what was once one of the more affluent areas of East Tarentum, PA and took possession of a comfortable home on East 6th Avenue.

A bit after they moved in, he became aware of a seepage problem in his basement. Not wanting to bear the expense of a major project replete with backhoes, cement trucks, and so on, he decided to fix it himself by diverting ground water away from the foundation. This was a labor intensive solution, but it did save quite a bit of money.

One day, while he was cutting sod and digging at the back of his home, his shovel struck an object that gave off a slight "clink" sound when it was hit. He got down on his hands and knees and retrieved an ancient blue glass bottle with its cork intact. It even contained some residue of its original contents.

A short while later, a nearby elderly neighbor engaged him in some friendly conversation and happened to notice the bottle.

"You know what you've got there?" he asked

"A really old glass bottle," Bill replied.

"Not just that, but it is a Laudanum bottle and still has some in it. Do you know what Laudanum is?"

Bill replied that, if he remembered correctly, it was an opium mixture that was used for a large number of ailments in the 19th and early 20th centuries.

"Right you are!" the old fellow said. "You've got a good find there. Maybe it's worth some money to a collector."

And the conversation headed off in a new direction. They discussed things like the weather and the demise of the steel industry in the valley and so on.

Eventually the neighbor asked him if he noticed anything unusual about his house.

"Like what?" Bill asked.

"Oh you know. Things out of the ordinary, weird things, strange lights, and so on," The fellow replied.

"Why do you ask?"

"Well, before you bought the place, it was empty for quite a while. From time-to-time, when the wife and I were sitting on our back porch in the evening we saw lights flickering and moving back and forth inside the windows on the second floor. It was at night when we knew there was nobody supposed to be there."

"We've heard some sounds and things moving about at night, but we just figured it was the normal sounds of an old house settling in. Why?"

"You don't know the history of your home, do you?"

Bill confessed that he didn't and his neighbor asked him if he had ever heard of Evelyn Nesbit, the world's first super model.

"Just a little, from movie that was made about her in the 1950s," was his reply.

"Well Bill, Florence Evelyn Nesbit spent most of her childhood in that very same house. She was born Christmas Day 1884 or 1886 in another part of town. Then, when her father became more wealthy, the family moved into that house and stayed there until 1893.

Even as a baby and toddler, her beauty brought her fame and people would come from all around just to gaze on the face of this beautiful child. It was the happiest time of Evelyn's life with two doting parents who strived to see that she wanted for nothing.

In 1893, with the increased success of her father, an attorney, the family moved to Pittsburgh. But he died a couple of years after the move and left the family penniless. Her mother decided to capitalize on Evelyn's beauty.

and she was "discovered"

She became the first number one super model in the world before her 16th birthday. Her face and body adorned everything from playing cards to magazine covers. Her name was known in every household in the country as the most beautiful woman in the world. It started when she became a dancer in the chorus line of a Broadway show and was suddenly "discovered" by famous pen and ink artist Charles Dana Gibson. Before she knew it, she was in featured roles along the Great White Way and added the title of "Broadway Star" to her resume. She found herself wooed by millionaires and international stars alike, from the fabled John Barrymore to ultra-rich New York Architect Stanford White. All this for the little girl from the small industrial town of Tarentum, PA that had a population of 4,000. On top of it all, she was just 16 years old to hear her mother tell it. Some accounts said that she was only 14.

That's what Florence Evelyn Nesbit faced in 1901. After a lavish courtship, she was plied with champagne and lost her virginity to 47 year old Stanford White, called "Stanny," by his associates. He then passed her on to a friend of his, actor John Barrymore, who was 21 at the time. Smitten by her beauty and being an honorable man, he asked for her hand in marriage. Based on the advice of her mother who considered Mr. Barrymore's financial future as an actor to be uncertain, she turned him down.

Then she met Pittsburgh multimillionaire Henry Thaw and subsequently married him in 1905. Instead of an idyllic existence free from financial cares, she found herself a virtual prisoner in the Thaw Mansion, called Lyndhurst on Beechwood Boulevard in the Squirrel Hill section of the city.

Henry Thaw was obsessed with his wife's past showing symptoms of what today would be called paranoid schizophrenia fueled by a morphine addiction. On June 25, 1906, Henry Thaw and his young wife Evelyn attended a rooftop production of *Mam'zelle Champagne* at the Madison Square Garden. Also in attendance at a private table was Stanford White. During the closing production number, "I Could Love A Million Girls," Henry Thaw approached Stanford

White. Standing less than three feet away, he shot White three times in the head, obliterating his face.

Standing over Stanford White's dead body waving his pistol in the air, Henry Thaw addressed the crowd, shouting, "He ruined my wife!"

What followed was a media frenzy and a courtroom sideshow that was called, "The Trial of the Century," the first of many given that appellation. Judged criminally insane, Henry Thaw was sentenced to an asylum in upstate New York. After seven years, his wealth managed to get him judged sane and he walked out a free man. He died in 1947 leaving his wife $10,000 of his $1,000,000+ estate.

The movie, *The Girl in the Red Velvet Swing,* released in 1955 and starring Joan Collins, Ray Milland, and Farley Grange was based on her early life and marriage. She served as technical adviser for the move and received a few thousand dollars for it

Evelyn finally passed on in 1967 after a career that never approached her earliest fame.

And this is what Bill learned about the unfortunate Evelyn. It seemed as though his home was the home of a famous celebrity's spirit who wanted to stay where she remembered her favorite time. Or at least the old man said so.

As years passed, Bill and other members of his family heard unexplained noises from time-to-time, one corner of the dining room was always as cold as the inside of a refrigerator, even in the summer, and the sweet smell of lilacs would waft on the air when there were no flowers present.

Bill learned that lilac was Evelyn's favorite flower and wore perfume of that aroma.

Hmm, Bill thought when these things would happen, *Maybe the old fellow has something after all.* Then he'd give his head a negative shake and return to reality.

The family cat had no problem believing. He'd arch his back, extend his fur to twice its regular size, then spit and hiss at something or someone no one else could see.

Bill's family grew and his daughter, Michelle matured into a beautiful young woman herself, attracting the attention of local young men. One in particular, Heath, became her steady beau and was a household fixture, accepted as one of the family.

One evening in particular, when the hour grew late, he asked for permission to sleep over, rather than head home at such an hour. Bill readily gave him that permission, with one caveat: he had to sleep on the couch in the downstairs living room while Michelle slept upstairs in her own room. Satisfied with the arrangement, the family settled down, the home grew quiet, and everyone surrendered themselves to the spell of Morpheus, Greek God of Dreams.

In the morning, as the family gathered round the kitchen table for breakfast, Bill asked Heath how he enjoyed his sleep on the couch.

Came the answer, "The couch was comfortable enough, but I will never sleep another night in this house!"

"Why so?" Bill asked.

"Well," he told him, "Everything was fine at first. The couch was quite comfy and I settled in for a nice night's sleep. But some time around 3 or 4 in the morning, I woke up. I don't even know what woke me, just something.

"Anyhow, I sat up and looked around to see what it was that woke me. I looked over to the stairs leading up to the second floor and saw a young lady walk down the stairs to the landing. She paused on the landing and I saw that she was wearing a long filmy nightgown of some sort or another.

"I thought it was Michelle and called out to her, but she didn't answer. She just continued down the stairs, and walked down the hall to the kitchen.

"I guessed that Michelle didn't hear me and was going into the kitchen for a middle of the night snack or something, so I followed her there. When I got to the kitchen, it was empty. Nobody was there. And nobody left the kitchen, either, I would have known.

"It must've been a ghost or something and I will never spend another night in this house!" he repeated himself with emphasis.

Ruminating on the event later, Bill

remembered his old neighbor's conversation word for word as though it had just happened. He and the rest of his family had been accepting the strangeness of the house until the day they moved in 2004.

He wondered if maybe, just maybe, the guy was right after all.

Encounter on Turkey Hill Mountain

Don't let Bethanie Mack's beauty fool you. Just because she has intrinsic beauty and a sense of compassion that exudes comfort and caring doesn't mean that she can't kick butt when necessary. Certain people who confused kindness with weakness found this out the hard way. This transplanted farm girl is equally at home in an evening gown as well as well-worn jeans. These days, however, she prefers to stay at home in a sweatsuit cuddling on the couch with her husband Warren.

As a teenager, Beth loved the outdoors and spent as much of her free time as possible exploring rural Somerset county on her single-seat quad-runner. One of her favorite rides was through the woods of the Stoystown area and up the flank of locally-named Turkey Hill Mountain. Once at the mesa on the top, she loved to look out over the never-ending rolling vista of Pennsylvania's tree covered hills and mountains.

On one outing, then sixteen year-old Beth was accompanied by a group of friends, six in all. Besides her quad, there was a pair each of quads 3-wheelers, and dirt bikes. The group rode the single track trails to the top of the mountain and paused to rest a bit. They had gotten a late start that day and evening was fast approaching when they summitted the hill. The mountain tops were starting to acquire that light purple haze that makes sunsets in the Pennsylvania highlands so beautiful.

After a bit, Beth noticed a peculiar smell wafting her way and mentioned it to the other riders. She says that she can only describe it as an overpowering combination of sweetness and muskiness combined with a cloying stickiness. She wasn't the only one to notice it. At first the consensus was that a large animal, like a deer, was rotting somewhere nearby. But, these were country kids and they knew what a rotting deer smelled like. This wasn't it. They looked about for the source of the odor and heard some disturbance in the brush a ways downhill. By now, evening had settled in and those who had them turned on their headlights for illumination.

Beth scanned the treeline with her headlights spotting the origin of the smell, and it terrified her. It was an animal-human hybrid of some kind that stood almost eight feet tall. She knew this because it was as high as the branches that she and her friends liked to swing on sometimes.

It was covered head to toe in medium length red fur interspersed with streaks of gray.

When the headlights of the 4-wheelers alighted on it, it turned and gave the group of youngsters a malevolent stare. Beth says she will never forget those deep, black pupil-less eyes that watched her with such hatefulness.

That was enough for her! Beth, possibly the bravest of the whole bunch, was the first one down the mountain to the relative safety of a paved road. She never rode her quad-runner on Turkey Hill Mountain again.

Sasquatch?

Bigfoot?

You be the judge, she's not going back to find out.

An Encounter With Big Bird

I've been relating stories told to me by
other people. Now here's one that actually
happened to me that I'd like to share with you.

On Wednesday, October 1, 2014 at
approximately 4:15PM, I was on my way home
from Blairsville, PA. I live in the small town of
New Florence in the Conemaugh Valley just
upstream from Packsaddle Gap. Although it is
only about 6 miles from Blairsville by way of the
railroad, it is nearly 20 miles by road. That's
because the only road access from that direction
is by going over the Chestnut Ridge on Longview
Mountain via US Route 22, then south on Pa
Route 259 to Milligan Hill Road, then up and
over Mulligan Hill. The top of Mulligan Hill is
plateau-like and planted with corn on the west
side of the road. To the east of the road, the
hillside falls away. Then the road drops about
200 feet over a space of 1/4 mile through a

wooded area to the bottom. The location is about 2 miles in a straight line from the New Florence Electric Generation Station and about 6 miles from the Seward Electric Generation Station.

Ok, the preceding is just background to give you an idea of location and place. Both the wooded area and the cornfields at the top of the hill are heavily populated with wild turkeys. Many times, while driving along this stretch of road, I have been startled by a wild turkey flying over my vehicle from one side of the road to another. I tell you this to let you know that I can easily identify a wild turkey in flight.

On this particular afternoon, the weather was clear and warm with a temperature in the mid 70s.

As I was driving down the slope heading south on Mulligan Hill Road, a large black shape flew over my vehicle nearly blotting out the sunlight. It was much larger than the largest wild turkey I'd ever seen. I cannot begin to identify the creature, I can only describe it.

It was either black or extremely dark

brown with an elongated neck similar to a goose or a heron and flew in a rising trajectory from east to west over the road. I think that its beak, which resembled that of a raptor was a light brown, but I'm not 100% sure. Its legs, which were tucked up into its body and trailing behind had talons and were also a light brown. The bird, if that's what it was, had an approximate wingspan of 12 feet and it was about 12 to 15 feet in length. It was completely covered in feathers and the trailing edge of the wings had feathers extending behind it, similar to the flaps on an airplane wing. Also, it may have been flying soundlessly, because I could not hear it over the sound of my car's engine and tires.

You may wonder how I was able to gather so much information and description in the short amount of time that it took to glide over my car. I can offer two reasons. One, it imprinted itself on my memory since it was such an unusual event. Two, the damn thing was no more than 15 feet above my car! I'm just glad that it was holding its bowels or it would have broken a window at least!

The Mirror

A middle-aged gentleman, obviously in great health and physical condition, along with his wife who was also into the healthy lifestyle bought both of my books about the hauntings along Pennsylvania roadways: *Pennsylvania's Haunted Route 30* and *Pennsylvania's Haunted Route 22.* Thumbing through the book about Route 30, he commented, "I see you missed one."'

That piqued my interest, so I asked' "How so?"

Here's what he told me -

Right off Route 30 in the Ligonier area was a house that dated all the way back to the 1830s. It was in such a deteriorated condition that it couldn't be restrored and was scheduled for demolition.

On a particularly sweltering August afternoon he noticed the workmen preparing the site, so he asked the supervisor wearing the white hard hat if he could look around.

"No skin off my nose," was the reply. He took this as tacit permission, so he and his wife went on in.

They were amazed to find a lot of the contents still in place. But most of them were just old, not antique, and in such a state of disrepair as to be only fit for kindling wood. It looked like squatters had been living in the house for some time. But the intrepid pair of "diggers" persevered, examining all the nooks and crannies they could find. Eventually that doggedness paid off when a closet yielded treasure.

Treasure to them, that is. To anybody else it was just a filigreed and gilded old mirror showing the patina of age. And dust, lots of dust.

"Honey, this mirror would be perfect for over the table in our foyer," she exclaimed.

He agreed. It fit the style of that old table and was the perfect size as well.

Sneezing in the cloud he created by blowing the dust layer from some of the filigreed decorations., he commented, "It'll go perfectly with that statue of Dad's that we put on that table."

Right here I interrupted his story to ask why he had a statue of his dad in the foyer.

He explained that it was a statue that had previously *belonged* to his dad, not a statue *of* his dad. That point cleared up, he continued.

He picked the mirror up and removed it from the closet. Suddenly the temperature dropped enough to give both of them a chill.

"Honey, let's get out of here," his wife demanded.

The old house was then filled with the sounds of doors and windows slamming shut.

He grabbed the mirror and they headed for the door which was now closed. They had to struggle with it to open it.

"Looks like the mirror doesn't want us to leave its home," he quipped.

They took the mirror home, cleaned it,

and gave it its place of honor in the foyer. But it brought with it a sense of foreboding and suspense. It looked great, but it made them uneasy whenever they looked into it.

"It's kind of hard to explain," he said. "It was always as though an unseen someone was looking over my shoulder when I looked into it, An unseen someone who bore me ill will. And I wasn't the only one who felt that way."

They decided that, even though the mirror fit so well into the foyer decor, it had to go. They decided to only keep it until they could find a replacement.

The mirror must have sensed their intentions because one day it "fell" from its place on the wall. As it fell, it struck the statue, cleaving the head from it as neatly as a guillotine. But the mirror survived the "fall" without damage not even scuffing the gilt.

They waited no longer and got rid of it immediately by donating it to a church based resale shop where, they hoped, its anger would be dissuaded.

Otherworldly Tales I've Been Told

About the Author

Ed Kelemen is an author, columnist, playwright and speaker who lives in a small west Central Pennsylvania town with his wife, two of five sons, a huge dog, and a clutch of attitude-ridden cats. His articles and short stories have appeared in numerous local, regional, and national publications. Visitors are always welcome at his website at www.ekelemen.com and he is easily found on Facebook.

Otherworldly Tales I've Been Told

Other Titles by Ed Kelemen

Pennsylvania's Haunted Route 30 - a travelogue of haunted places along US Route 30 from Pittsburgh to Philadelphia.*

Pennsylvania's Haunted Route 22 - 320 miles of haunted highway from Pittsburgh to Easton, PA

We Don't Talk About Those Kinds of Things - The Making of a Psychic - Written with Beverly LaGorga. Her development from a scared little girl who saw things that no one else could to an accolmplished psychic.

Twisted Tales from a Twisted Mind - A collection of stories of the macabre that originated in the strange psyche of the author.

The Little Drummer Girl of Gettysburg - A gentle ghost story for young readers as well as those who are young at heart.*

The Dutch Uncle - A novel about the adventures of Pittsburgh's newest P.I., P. T. O'Conner.*

All of these titles are available at local booksores as well as at Amazon.

* These are also available for Amazon Kindle.

32805042R10058

Made in the USA
Middletown, DE
18 June 2016